A PRIMER ON POLITICS BEFORE AND AFTER THE ELECTION

*PART ONE: THE CAMPAIGN IS
ALL ABOUT THE CANDIDATE.
PART TWO: THOUGHTS OF
AN ELECTED OFFICIAL*

BENJAMIN ALLEN

Order this book online at www.trafford.com
or email orders@trafford.com

Most Trafford titles are also available at major online book retailers.

Printed in the United States of America.

ISBN: 978-1-4907-3460-6 (sc)
ISBN: 978-1-4907-3459-0 (hc)
ISBN: 978-1-4907-3458-3 (e)

Library of Congress Control Number: 2014907708

Trafford rev. 04/28/2014

 www.trafford.com

North America & international
toll-free: 1 888 232 4444 (USA & Canada)
fax: 812 355 4082

CONTENTS

Part II

Thoughts of an Elected Official

About the Author

Benjamin Allen is a former state legislator. He has served as a political advisor for local and state campaigns. He has lectured on campaigning, and he frequently comments on politics on local television, radio, and in local print media.

FOREWORD

This book of elementary principles of politics is written in two (2) parts. Part I is entitled "The Campaign Is All about the Candidate." It is primarily concerned with matters to be considered by a person involved in a campaign. Part II is entitled "Thoughts of an Elected Official." It is primarily concerned with a reflection of what happens during a term in office when the campaigning ends and the work of representing the people begins.

This book is written in two (2) parts because all too often, a person running for public office is focused on winning an election, giving little or no thought to what happens when the campaigning ends and representing the people begins. What happens after the election, during the term in office, is just as important as to what happens before the election, during the campaign. This book, *A Primer on Politics before and after the Election* provides a guide for any person who wants to be a candidate and an elected official.

PART I

The Campaign Is All about the Candidate

Part I is about campaigning. There are no theories of campaigning presented, only practical information about campaigning.

Part I gives practical information to candidates, volunteers, and paid staff for a campaign and to others who want to know about campaigning. The information is helpful for those running a campaign that has little or no money and is helpful for those running a campaign with lots of money to spend on a campaign. This part gives practical information to those involved in any campaign, regardless of the size of the campaign.

Part I should be read by anyone who is interested in political campaigns, not just those who are actively involved in campaigning.

After reading Part I there will be one single fact that stands out about campaigning, and that is "campaigning is all about the candidate."

CHAPTER 1

Being a Leader Is Not Easy

Public officials are leaders by way of their "elected" position.

There are people who become leaders by happenstance. They are usually community organizers who are known in the community for advocating either in support of or in opposition to a community interest. Citizens in the community began to seek out the community organizer for help because citizens see the community organizer as a leader.

Sometimes a community organizer decides that he can best advocate for a community interest by being a public official.

Being a leader, whether elected or appointed, is not easy. Every decision a leader makes is second-guessed. No leader has support of 100 percent of his followers; he will not even have the support of 100 percent of his supporters. The leader will have those who want him to fail. And some naysayers will actively campaign for the failure of the leader.

There will be times a leader will question his reasons for wanting to lead. This is so because even when a leader does good, his motive for doing good will be criticized and second-guessed. There will be those who will say the leader's action is selfish even when the leader's action is pure.

Nevertheless, a leader must do good; a leader must do what is right.

The role of a leader is not to win a popularity contest; a position of leadership demands taking a stance on issues that will best serve the community interest. Sometimes the right stance to be taken is not the popular stance. Martin Luther King, Jr. once stated that "the ultimate measure of a man is not where he stands in moments of comfort and convenience but where he stands at times of challenge and controversy."[1] And, so it is with a leader. The leader must not be afraid to challenge the prevailing view, if it is wrong. A leader must do what is right. The leader's enthusiasm, loyalty, and devotion must always be on the side of "what is right" for those whose trust the leader has been given.

If one chooses to lead by holding an elective office, he has an option. He can be a politician holding an elective office, or he can be a public servant occupying a position of trust given to him by the community. There is a difference between a politician and a public servant. The politician is like a paper bag being blown by the wind; he takes no position on any matters of interest in the community, he is pushed about by the winds of complaints. The public servant takes a position on a matter of interest in the community; he is mindful of the opinions of others, and the opinions are part of the information used to reach a decision. The public servant does not seek comfort or convenience when making a decision; he seeks to insure that any decision reached is "what is right." He seeks to insure that any decision reached is fair and just.

---

[1] *The Words of Martin Luther King, Jr.*, New York: Newmarket Press, 1983, 1987, & 1996, p. 24

CHAPTER **2**

The Challenge to Do Something

The first question to be answered when considering a "run" for public office is, why do I want to be an elected official? This is a personal question. The question must be answered, and it must be answered truthfully.

The idea for running for public office may originate with someone other than the candidate; nevertheless, the decision to run must be the candidate's decision.

A former legislator tells the story of how he made his decision to run for public office, following a challenge given to him by his father.

The former legislator had completed his studies at the university. He had returned home to begin his work-life.

One day, the former legislator attended a community meeting. He was concerned about what was said at the community meeting. He told his father about the meeting and those matters he heard at the community meeting. In the conversation with his father, he repeated over and over the phrase "somebody ought to do something."

At the end of the visit with his father, as the former legislator was reaching for the front door, his father, who was walking to the door with him, grabbed his arm, looked him in the eyes, and asked, "Are you that somebody? Are you that somebody that we have been talking about this evening? Will you do something about the matters you care so passionately about?" The former legislator paused to consider the words of his father. Before he could respond, his father said in a calm reassuring tone, "I believe you are that somebody; be that somebody, do something."

On the night of his election, the former legislator recalled the story of the evening he shared his concerns with his father and his father's challenge to him to "be that somebody" and "do something." He told his audience that he accepted the challenge to run so that he could use the elected office to "do something" about the community concerns that was discussed at that community meeting.

CHAPTER **3**

Beginning the Campaign

Before starting a campaign, you must answer the question, do I have the support of my family? You must consider the wishes of your family before committing to a campaign, because the family will be affected by the campaign. The campaign will demand your undivided attention. For example, family time will be affected by the campaign. You will not be around for family events; you will be campaigning. You will miss family events because the campaign comes first. You will use family money to fund the campaign. Your family members must be told of the needs of the campaign and the family members must be willing to accept the fact that the campaign will affect the family.

Obtaining family support does not mean you can ignore the family needs doing the campaign. You must find a way to balance the demands of the campaign and the needs of the family. The failure to balance the competing interests could prove to be disastrous for you; you could lose both your family and the election.

You must get family members involved in the campaign by giving those who want to work a specific job (when possible). It is better to have family members actively involved in the campaign than being on the outside, looking in. Your family members must accept the campaign as being their campaign. And, if they do, they will be your best supporters and campaign workers.

After obtaining the support of family members, you must identify key advisors, persons who will be members of the steering committee to develop a strategy for the campaign. A member of the steering committee must have experience working in a political campaign; and if astute in political matters, this person should be the campaign's political consultant. One member of the steering committee must be the chairperson for the campaign. And, a member of the steering committee must be the campaign's treasurer.

You must meet with your steering committee weekly. (See Appendix B for Eight Things to Know about Steering Committee Meetings.) The first task of you and your advisors is to gather information on federal, state, and local election laws. You must know the requirements of the office, such as, "What is the residency requirement of the office?"; and "What are the reporting requirements of the office you are seeking to hold?" The failure to know and follow the requirements of office could end a campaign before it begins. One member of the steering committee should be given the responsibility of insuring that the campaign complies with election laws.

Before publicly announcing your candidacy, you must know why you are running for office, and you must be able to articulate your reason(s) for running. The members of the steering committee must meet and assist with preparing the announcement to insure you will not stumble when making the announcement. You must look and sound like you are ready to take office when you stand before the public, including the media, to announce you are running for office. (See Appendix A for an example of a candidate's to-do list, showing things a candidate must do to run a campaign.)

CHAPTER 4

One Last Check before Beginning the Campaign

Running a campaign is hard work. It is both time consuming and expensive. Knowing this, and before announcing your candidacy and during the process to decide whether to run or not run, you must take a hard look at yourself. You must decide whether there are skeleton(s) in your closet that will affect the campaign. Your personal, financial, and professional records must not present any questionable lapses in judgment that will prove to be embarrassing during the campaign. Your general reputation in the community must be "good." A campaign can be brought to an end by what is "in the closet" of a candidate.

This does not mean you must be a saint, a perfect person, to run for public office; there may be matters of concern about your past and you still run for public office. It simply means that anything in the your past that may potentially be a problem must be made known to your key advisors and your family before the decision to run is made. Your past misstep should not be a surprise (something learned from one other than you) to those closest to you.

If there is a reasonable explanation for the matter of concern, then it will not become a distraction, dominating the campaign; if this is so, even though you have a less than perfect past you may run without fear of your past being a possible problem for the campaign.

Further, if the matter of concern is one that happened when you were of a youthful age (depending upon community norms, one under the age of twenty-five could be considered youthful), the voting public will probably forgive you attributing the misstep to youthful indiscretion. This is particularly so if you have had no other missteps and you have been a good citizen in the community since having the misstep.

Whether or not a past problem should stop you from running for public office depends upon how well you are prepared to handle questions about the misstep (this is the reason for discussing the misstep with close advisors so that the advisors can assist with preparing a response to questions about the misstep) and what you have done in the community since the misstep. You must be honest and forthright when speaking about the misstep. You must not offer any excuses for the misstep. You must be able to show that in spite of the misstep, you have moved beyond the misstep and become a positive contributing member of the community.

Of course, if you have had multiple missteps, the voting public will probably be less likely to support your candidacy.

CHAPTER **5**

The Campaign Is about the Candidate

Regardless of the size of a campaign, all campaigns are the same. The campaign is driven by the candidate and fueled by volunteers. A campaign depends heavily on the passion of the candidate; it is the candidate, not volunteers and not money that will determine the course of a campaign. And, the candidate's passion will weigh heavily on the outcome of the campaign.

When you qualify to be the candidate, you are responsible for the campaign.

When things go right, you will get credit that you do not deserve. When things go wrong, you will get blame that you do not deserve.

When you qualify to be the candidate, you are the face of the campaign. The campaign will be all about you. But yet, you must remember not to take yourself too serious. There will be times when laughter is appropriate even when it occurs at your expense.

Qualifying to be the candidate does not mean you have been given a monopoly on all good ideas. You will need the help of others. You must be willing to ask for, solicit, the help of others. And you must be willing to accept and use the help of others to chart the course of the campaign and to run the campaign.

You must be quick to praise others for work done for the campaign. And, you must be slow to criticize those who do not meet your expectations when completing a task for the campaign.

You must be willing to finance the campaign with your time, talents, and treasure.

You must believe in the message of the campaign.

And, you must believe in yourself. You must believe that you are as good as anyone, but you must never believe you are better than anyone.

You must have principles to live by, but you cannot be so principled that you cannot live.

In short, the campaign deals with your personality, credibility, and charisma; the outcome of the campaign is driven by your hard work; and is fueled by the passion of your supporters.

CHAPTER **6**

The Candidate Must Make Decisions

There are decisions to be made by you about the campaign. Some decisions are easy to make and others are difficult; even those difficult, tough decisions must be made by you. You should not ask others in the campaign to make the tough decisions that must be made nor should you expect others to make the tough decisions for your campaign.

Before making a decision, it is important that information is gathered to make the decision. You must ask questions; you must understand what is being asked, and you must understand the consequences of your decision.

You must consult with members of the steering committee, since the help of the steering committee will be needed to support any decision made.

Before making any decision, you should get enough information to make the decision a good decision, one supported by fairness and justice. You should not be afraid to make any needed adjustments after making a decision if the adjustments will make the decision a better decision.

There are important decisions that you must make affecting those you have put in leadership positions to help run the campaign. Those chosen must be allowed to do their job. You must trust those who are put in leadership positions to work for the campaign. However, if a person put in a leadership position does not have the time to complete a given task, or has shown an unwillingness to be a "team player," you must quickly make a decision to remove that person from the leadership position. Team work is needed to successfully run a campaign. Your failure to make timely decisions concerning the campaign's leadership, such as removing a person who is unfit to lead, could adversely affect the outcome of the election. The campaign requires workers, and if those in leadership positions do not work or is unwilling to work, then those who are not in leadership positions will not be inspire to work resulting in no work being done for the campaign. And if no work is done for the campaign, you will not win the campaign.

CHAPTER 7

The Candidate's Steering Committee

You must identify who you want to be a part of the steering committee. The steering committee of the campaign should be composed of your most trusted advisors, who will be called upon to look at the campaign—identifying strengths and weaknesses—helping you to chart a course for the running of the campaign.

The steering committee should include the following persons: political consultant, treasurer, campaign chairperson, and other coordinators. You must meet with the steering committee to plan the campaign. Ideally there will be several meeting with the steering committee before you make a public announcement that you are running for a public office.

It is your responsibility to name advisors, and when doing so, you must select individuals for their loyalty to you and their commitment to running a winning campaign. It is a plus for a member of the steering committee to have prior political experience working with a political campaign, but the failure of any member to have prior political experience is not a matter that the campaign cannot overcome; you can purchase the services of a political consultant to assist with the campaign.

While you can purchase the services of a political consultant, you cannot purchase loyalty and commitment. Loyalty and commitment of supporters must be earned by you. You must show concern and be conscious of your relationship with your supporters before, and during, and after the campaign. As the campaign moves forward, you will learn that loyalty and commitment of supporters are needed to keep supporters actively engaged in the campaign and are a must to bring the enthusiasm needed for the campaign to be effective in obtaining enough votes on Election Day for you to win.

You must trust the members of the steering committee to work for the campaign. If a steering committee member does not have the time to complete a given task, you must not hesitate to remove that member from the steering committee. You must be forever mindful that things don't just happen; work is required to make things happen, and if a member is not willing to work, then the member must be removed and replaced by a person willing to work.

(See Appendix D for an example of a campaign organizational chart.)

CHAPTER **8**

The Candidate Must Have a Plan

When considering what must be done, the thought of campaigning will appear to be overwhelming. It will help to departmentalize what must be done by using a calendar and a timeline to plan campaign events. You must plan today for tomorrow. A calendar showing the timeline for events must be created. (See Appendix C for an example of a timeline for use by a campaign.) You should not let time control the campaign, rather you must control the time needed for the campaign. And by doing so, you will not be overwhelmed by what must be done.

If you want to win your election, then you must plan to win the election. Proper planning requires that you organize events in a manner that will lead to the results desired. Your campaign plan must have events that will give life to the campaign. Every event should be for the purpose of getting 50 percent plus one of the votes cast on Election Day. Care should be taken to build momentum in the campaign, with excitement peaking on Election Day.

You must develop a plan to get your name into the conscious of the voters. The plan must raise your name recognition so that the voters will know you and vote for you.

You must know the district that you are seeking to represent. And, you must know the voters.

In addition to knowing who the voters are, you must know what the voters in the district are saying about the role of government.

Knowing the voters will help you to develop a message that will be heard by the voters in the district. Your campaign message must be simple, and it must state to the voters reasons why they should vote for you.

In addition to having a message, your use of a simple memorable campaign slogan will help you raise your name recognition.

To further help you raise your name recognition, you must create a logo and color scheme to be used by the campaign. Your slogan and logo must complement each other, and they must be consistent with the campaign message. The purpose of the campaign slogan and logo is to inform the voters of who you are, to define your candidacy; and the campaign message must convince the voters to vote for you on Election Day.

In addition to knowing who the voters are and what the voters are saying about the role of government, you must know who the "actual voters" (those who regularly vote in elections) are in the district. You must target the "actual voters." The "actual voters" must know you and must commit to vote for you.

The campaign must target voters, seek out those voters who have a similar interest about the role of government as you do. It is the voters who have similar interests as you that will most likely support your candidacy by doing volunteer work for the campaign and voting for you. You must make a strong effort to contact these voters.

In some elections, contacting voters can be done by you going door-to-door, covering by foot the voting district. If the voting district can be covered by foot, you should "walk the voting district." You should go door-to-door, greeting voters and asking for their vote. Personal contact with voters is the most effective method of campaigning. Voters want to meet you. Voters want to be asked for their vote(s). And, if the voters have questions, they want you to personally answer the questions.

In those elections where it is impossible for you to cover the voting district by foot, going door-to-door, you should visit areas, places where people gather in large numbers in the voting district and meet the voters. Voters want you to visit their community; and when possible, you must visit a community and ask the voters for their vote.

Even when you cannot go door-to-door, you should have your supporters going door-to-door in the voting district, greeting the voters and asking them to support your candidacy by voting for you.

Contact raising your name recognition can be done by putting up yard signs, by putting up billboards, by using mail-out, by using effectively the media, running radio and television ads, by doing public-speaking engagements, and by having a web page.

It is important for you to be familiar with the concerns of the community that you want to represent. Even though you may be a lifelong resident of a community, you may not be familiar with what is "being said on the streets by residents about a community concern." You must find a way to become familiar with what is being said on the streets.

You must be visible in the community. You should visit those places in the community where politics is being discussed. And, you must listen to the political debates of the residents at those locations, political hot spots, such as barbershops, beauty salons and popular restaurants.

As a part of the campaign, you must visit community leaders, both elected and appointed. And, you must listen to the political comments made.

To gather information about the community and about what is being said about you in the community, you must subscribe to the media, print, radio, television, and Internet, providing news coverage for the community. And, you must listen to what is being said about the community and about you. And the information obtained should be used to develop and run your campaign.

Sometimes, it may be in the campaign's best interest to conduct a poll on a particular question. The poll can be formal or informal. You can hire a pollster to do a survey and report the findings on a question. Or, you can do an informal poll; having persons to go out into the community, asking the question of those they meet on the street, and reporting their findings back to you for use in the development and running your campaign.

You should use the Internet to reach the voters with the campaign message. And you should the use the Internet to conduct polls to gather information on questions of community interest.

In short, you must move about the community; you must stop and listen to anyone who is willing to talk to you about community concerns and about you. The information gathered, including polling information, is to be used to assist with developing a plan to run the campaign.

CHAPTER **9**

I Am the Candidate—
The Announcement

You must stage the public announcement to run for office. You should have key advisors (steering committee) and other supporters present for the announcement. The media must be present for the announcement. And the announcement should be broadcast to your web page.

At least forty-eight hours prior to the date of the announcement, you must notify the media with a press release of the pending announcement. The press release must state the date, time, and place of the announcement; the office that you are seeking should be stated in the press release, and a short statement of who you are should be stated in the press release (a one-page document). (See Appendix F for an example of a candidate's news kit to be sent to news media outlets prior to the candidate's public announcement.)

The announcement should be held at a location that is symbolic of your run for office. For example, if your campaign will rely heavily on matters of education, then the announcement should be made on the steps of the local board of education.

The announcement program should last no more than fifteen to twenty minutes. Other than the campaign chairperson making an endorsement of your candidacy and introducing you, there should be one other speaker and that speaker is you.

You should announce in a short, concise simple statement that you are running for office. The statement made by you at the announcement must answer four questions, namely:

1. Who are you?
2. Why are you running for office?
3. What makes you qualified to hold office?
4. What is the campaign about?

You should make a written copy of the statement made at the announcement and a short biography of you (a one-page document) available for the media.

The announcement serves several purposes. It is a time for you to contact the community to gain name recognition, answering the question, "Who am I? It is an opportunity for you to define who you are and to get your message to the community, defining the campaign.

CHAPTER **10**

The Candidate Must Tell a Story

You have made your announcement; you have told your family, friends, and supporters that you are officially a candidate for office. At the announcement, there is excitement about your candidacy, the upcoming campaign, and what could be if you are elected. It is important for you to build on the momentum created by the announcement by having a plan in place for running the campaign, which must be implemented following the announcement.

However, before implementing the plan, you must immediately meet with your steering committee to review the announcement; questions need to be asked and answered. You must know what was done right, and you must know what could have been done better; you must know whether the announcement will convince 50 percent plus one of the voters to vote for you on Election Day.

Also, you and the steering committee must discuss what role the media will play in the campaign. A consensus needs to be reached on how the campaign can use the media to tell your story. Why make a fuss about the media? Simply put, if the media likes you, you will get "favorable" and "free" coverage helping the story of your candidacy to reach the voters at no monetary cost to you.

It is necessary for you to have a good, friendly working relationship with the media. Members of the media can be helpful in getting your message to the voting public. You want "good" press coverage. The best way to insure "good" press coverage is for you to be friendly with members of the media. If the media views you as being friendly and approachable, then stories written about you will be done in a favorable light, even if the media disagrees with the message.

You should obtain the services of a media specialist, a campaign spokesperson, to assist with the media needs of the campaign.

To be an effective candidate, you must learn to talk in "short sound bites." The media has limited time and space to devote to any campaign. To insure your campaign message is covered by the media, you must be able to answer questions in a short, clear, concise manner; you should not give rambling answers. If you do not have an answer, you should not hesitate to say, "I don't know," and you should assure the media that an answer will be forthcoming.

When talking with the media, your statements should be consistent with the message of the campaign.

The campaign message should appear on all campaign literature. The campaign message should be simple. The campaign message must be clear. Voters should not have to guess about the message of the campaign.

No one will know of your campaign unless the campaign message is heard and you are seen. You must be seen, and the campaign message must be heard by the voters. You can be seen, and the campaign message can be heard with the effective use of the media, print, and audiovisual, telling your story; you must use the Internet to reach voters; the campaign must have a web page, and your story must be told on the web page.

When telling your story, there are four rules to follow:

1. Know your audience.
2. Know the purpose of the story.
3. Keep the story simple.
4. Tell your story.

Who is the audience that the campaign is trying to reach? The campaign is reaching out to the citizens of the voting district; more particularly, the campaign is reaching out to the voters who live in the voting district. The message of the campaign must target the voters of the voting district.

What is the purpose of the message? You are running a campaign to get elected to a public office. To get elected, you need 50 percent plus one of the votes cast on Election Day. The purpose of the message is to convince 50 percent plus one of the voters on Election Day to vote for you.

The message of the campaign must be short. It must be consistently given. It must be easily understood and must be concise. It must have a "meaning." It must be a simple one.

The message is your story. It is a story of who you are, and it must show that you support the interest of the voting district. The story should convey both an actual message and a subtle message. The actual message is the campaign statement of support for the interest of the voting district. The subtle message is to create an air of confidence about you that has the effect of moving the voters to see you not just as a candidate, but as the best candidate to be the voting district representative because you support the interest of the voting district. Your subtle message(s) heard by the voters should be:

1. You can trust me.
2. I will not abuse your trust.
3. I am capable of getting the job done.
4. I am your champion.
5. I am just like you.

Subtle message(s) are just as important as the actual message of the campaign. You must work to craft subtle message(s) that will compliment the actual message(s) of the campaign.

The candidate's story is best told by you. Throughout the campaign, you must tell your story. You must remind the voters of who you are, and you must always state your support for the interest of the voting district, being consistent, concise, and purposeful when doing so.

The question is often asked, "Should the candidate answer a question based on the audience standing in front of him?" The answer is the audience should not be a factor, deciding whether a candidate will answer "yes" or "no" to a question. If an answer is, "yes" it will be "yes" no matter who is in the audience. However, the explanation accompanying the answer may change depending upon who is in the audience. You must take care to insure the voter will understand any position taken, even if the voter may disagree with the answer.

If you have not taken a position on a question, you should say so to the voters. And you should be open to studying the question to find an answer.

CHAPTER 11

The Candidate Must Obtain Endorsements

You can raise your name recognition by obtaining endorsements of individuals and organizations in the community. You must call upon community leaders; both elected and appointed, and ask for their public support. You must call upon community organizations and ask for their public support. The public support of individuals and organizations, if given, will have the effect of persuading those persons who support the individuals and organizations endorsing you to support you. By using the endorsement you are saying to the voters you know my endorser; my endorser supports this community; my endorser knows me; therefore you know me, and you know I care about our community. And you can trust me with your vote.

Just as an endorsement can be helpful, it can also be harmful. By receiving an endorsement you may be forced to take on the enemies of the individual or organization giving the endorsement. Knowing this, you must decide whether the cost of the endorsement is greater than the benefit; if the cost is greater than the benefit, then you should not seek or accept the endorsement.

You must seek and obtain only endorsements that are consistent with the message of the campaign and those that will enhance your campaign. You should not accept an endorsement of any individual or organization that will cause any voter to question the campaign message based on your association with one giving you an endorsement.

Any endorsement sought must be one that will help you to get 50 percent plus one of the votes cast on Election Day.

CHAPTER **12**

The Campaign Must Have a Slogan

To help you to tell your story, you should develop and use a campaign slogan.

The campaign slogan must be catchy and concise, and it must convey the campaign message loud and clear. The slogan should say who you are and what the campaign is all about, and it must subtly encourage the voters to vote for you, because you are "job ready"; and because you are job ready, you are the best candidate.

The slogan should be a simple sentence.

Developing a slogan can be a challenge. You must resist the temptation to be wordy when developing a slogan. Using too many words will be difficult for the voters to remember. The slogan is to be a saying that will stick in the minds of the voters.

A candidate who had previous experience as an elected official in a campaign used the slogan, "A proven leader with experience and integrity." This is a simple sentence, which says a lot about the candidate. The slogan tells the voters that the candidate is job ready; he is "a proven leader." It tells the voters that the candidate has legislative experience; he is "with experience." And, it tells the voters that the candidate can be trusted; he has "integrity." This slogan meets the criteria of a good campaign slogan, because it says a lot about the candidate in one short, simple sentence.

CHAPTER **13**

Know the Opposition

Even though your campaign should be run based on what you do best, you must know your opposition. Knowing the opposition means doing opposition research to gather information about the opposition. Once information is gathered about the opposition, the question becomes, what should be done with the information?

1. Should negative information from the opposition's closet be used in a negative campaign against the opposition to discredit the opposition? Or
2. Should the opposition's position on the issue(s) of the campaign that are different from yours be made known to the voters to persuade the voters to support you? Or
3. Should information about the opposition's education, work experience, association, income, etc., be used to predict how the opposition is likely to respond during the campaign?

You should be careful not to use the information gathered to make the campaign about discrediting the opposition based on the personal shortcomings. The campaign should be about "issues and ideas" to improve the general welfare of those living in the community. The campaign should not be about waging a negative campaign to discredit the opposition on essentially personal matters. This does not mean you should not highlight the opposition's position on the issues and ideas of the campaign; you must highlight for the voters the differences you and the opposition have on the issues and ideas of the campaign. Discrediting the opposition on the issues and ideas is acceptable campaigning. You want the voters to know the opposition is who he says he is and that the opposition's position on the issues and ideas of the campaign will not promote the general welfare of the community.

Knowing the opposition does not mean using the information gathered to determine whether the opposition is a "weak candidate." You should not run a campaign, believing little campaigning is needed on the belief that the opposition is a "weak candidate." There is no such thing as a "weak candidate." If a person meets the qualifications to run for office, that person is a worthy opponent; he is capable of getting sufficient votes to win an election. Accordingly, you should treat any opponent as a worthy opponent capable of winning an election. The campaign must work hard to insure you get 50 percent plus one of the votes cast on Election Day. You must give your best effort no matter who the opposition is; you must never underestimate the opposition.

CHAPTER **14**

Join a Political Party

Some candidates choose a political party based on personalities, answering the question, do I want to be associated with those persons who are members of the party? The likeability of those associated with a political party will attract the candidate. If the leader(s) of a party are not likeable, then it is less likely that a candidate will be drawn to the party represented by such leader(s). On the other hand, those leader(s) with charisma, likeable personalities will attract the candidate.

And, there are candidates who choose a political party based on the issues and ideas, answering the question, do I agree with those ideas and principles of the party? If the candidate agrees with the party's position on issues and ideas, then the candidate will want to be a member of the party. The candidate will want to help make the party's position on issues and ideas the position of government by joining, or becoming a member of, the political party and working to get those in government to support the position of the political party.

No candidate will agree with the political party's positions on all the issues and ideas all of the time. At best, what is hoped is that the candidate and the political party of the candidate can agree on most issues.

Knowing that there will be times of disagreement with the political party, you may ask, "Is being affiliated with a political party really necessary?" Whether you are running in a partisan or a nonpartisan race, joining a political party is important for several reasons. First, most political parties have a database of voters, supporters, contributors, and campaign workers that is made available to a candidate affiliated with the party. The information contained in the database is priceless for the savings in time and costs to you to develop the same information database.

When using a database, you must tailor the information to fit your needs. You must target those persons who you believe will most closely identify with you; those will be the persons who are most likely to vote for you, contribute to the campaign, and work for the campaign.

Because members of a political party can help with developing a campaign strategy, you should be a member of a political party. You must meet with party leaders and supporters. The help of party leaders and supporters to identify the strengths and weaknesses of the party and its members will be helpful in assisting you to develop a campaign strategy to insure you get the best information and workers to help your campaign.

Being affiliated with a political party will help you to develop name recognition. The political party has a recognizable brand in the community. The voters know from years of watching a political party what type of candidates the political party supports. The voters will assume any candidate associated with the political party will be similar to those who (past and present) are associated with the political party. And the voters know from years of watching a political party what position the political party (*by its work in the community*) has taken on an issue of concern in the community. The voters will assume any candidate associated with the political party will take the political party's position on any issue of concern in the community. And, if the voters in the past have supported candidates of a political party, those voters will be more likely support you if you are associated with the political party.

There is a negative to joining a political party. And, that is those who are opposed to the leadership and/or ideas of the political party will oppose you based on your membership in the party. Nevertheless, if you believe the positives of being a member of a party are greater than the negatives of being a member of a party, you should join a political party to help with your campaign.

CHAPTER **15**

The Candidate Must Resist Negative Ads

Sometime campaigns become mud-slinging contests, campaigns about the personal shortcomings of the candidates as opposed to a discussion of issues, ideas, and answering questions that the voters want answered. Should the opposition begin to campaign using negative statements about you; what should be your response? If you respond, should you respond by making negative statements about the opposition? Or, should you respond?

There will be supporters who will urge you to respond with "negative, attack ads" about the opposition. There will be supporters who will urge you to ignore the opposition's "negative, attack ads." You may be tempted to respond without considering the pros and cons of responding; you should never respond without discussing whether to respond, and how to respond, with your steering committee.

You must remember very few, if any, "negative attack ads" deserve a response. And more importantly, you must remember that voters do not like negative campaigning; negative campaigning could backfire with the voters sympathizing with the candidate being attacked, should the voters believe he is being unfairly attacked by a "negative attack ad."

You should take care when you are confronted with the one "negative attack ad" that you believe deserve a response. The campaign would be better served if you ignored the "negative attack ad," and continued with the campaign, emphasizing your platform and your position on the issues and ideas of the campaign. The goal of the campaign is not to fight with the opposition; it is to get 50 percent plus one of the votes on Election Day. The voters must be convinced that you can be trusted to govern in a fair and just manner if elected office; fighting the opposition on matters of no interest to the voters will not convince the voters you are fair or just and it will not get you 50 percent plus one of the votes on Election Day.

While providing negative comments about an opponent may produce laughter among voters, and it may get you a few votes, the negative comments will not determine the outcome of an election. Negative comments may cause voters to forget the campaign message. Or, the voters may confused the campaign message with the negative comments about the opposition, resulting in them not knowing what the campaign message is, making the negative comments the campaign message. This confusion will frustrate voters, resulting in a loss of votes for your candidacy.

The campaign is about your candidacy and your position on the issues and ideas of the campaign; it is not about fighting with the opposition with "negative attack ads."

CHAPTER **16**

The Candidate Must Delegate

You should not be so busy managing the day-to-day activities of the campaign that you forget to campaign or cannot campaign. You are the face of the campaign; you must be in and about the community campaigning through Election Day. You must be free to campaign and get out and meet the voters. You must be free from the demands of managing the day-to-day operation of the campaign. You must have help to manage the campaign; a campaign chairperson and an office manager are needed to manage the day-to-day activities of the campaign staff.

While it may be necessary for the campaign to have a paid staff to carry out certain functions of the campaign, the majority of the campaign staff will be volunteers. When developing a staff, the campaign must be mindful of a statement made by Clarence Francis: "You can buy a man's time; you can buy his physical presence at a given place; you can even buy a measured number of his skilled muscular motions per hour. But you cannot buy enthusiasm . . . you cannot buy loyalty . . . you cannot buy the devotion of hearts, minds, or souls. You must earn these."[2] It is not enough to have only the time of workers in a campaign; the passion of the workers is also needed. Your supporters must be excited about the campaign and your election to office.

You must work hard to earn the respect of your supporters. You must treat those who come to help you with honor and respect. And, you must be fair and just in all your dealings with those who work for the campaign. By being respectful with your supporters, you will earn their devotion and passion for the campaign.

You must ask supporters to volunteer to do the work to run the campaign. The campaign will never have enough money to pay all workers in the campaign. A majority of the work of the campaign will be done by volunteers. Accordingly it is important that you attract and keep volunteers. There are several keys to attracting and keeping volunteers, and they are as follows:

1. Never waste a volunteer's time.
2. Make reasonable work assignment for volunteers.
3. Welcome suggestions from volunteers.
4. Always thank the volunteer for being a part of the campaign.

As leader of your campaign, you must know the time demands of activities; you should not take too much of the volunteer's time. Similarly, you must recognize what activity a volunteer is best suited to carry out, and you must listen to suggestions of the volunteer when making a work assignment. You must keep the volunteer busy with activities that will get the vote out for you on Election Day. And finally, you must "thank" the volunteer. As a part of the fundraising efforts of the campaign, the campaign must have an event that serves as a money-making activity and as a means to say "thank you" to the volunteers.

---

[2]   www.world of quotes.com

CHAPTER **17**

The Candidate Must Raise Money

Not only must you be available to campaign to encourage others to support your candidacy as volunteers and to support your candidacy with a vote, but you must also raise money for the campaign.

A campaign costs "real money." It takes money to run a campaign. Money is needed to get name recognition, to get the campaign message to the voters, and to get the voters to the poll on Election Day.

While it takes money to run a campaign, an office cannot be bought. A good candidate with some money is still the best bet to win an election than a bad candidate with lots of money.

You must spend your money to support the campaign. You cannot expect others to use their money for the needs of the campaign when you do not contribute any money to support the campaign.

A campaign must establish a budget for use of money raised. The campaign must stay within the budget. When considering cost, the campaign must remember "man power" has a value. And sometimes "man power" must be purchased. When considering cost, the campaign must remember that overspending will not result in additional votes; there is a dollar amount when spent will be sufficient to get the votes needed to win. It is your responsibility to know when the dollar amount has been reached.

Effective fundraising begins and ends with you. People give money to the candidate. While the message is important and some donors will give based on the message, most donors give to the candidate. Accordingly you are the most important fundraiser for the campaign.

You must ask for money to run the campaign. This can be done by you asking for money using face-to-face solicitations, telephone solicitations, radio and television solicitations, direct mail, and computer solicitations using the campaign's website. Additionally, money can be raised using events, such as a small or large gathering (for example, fish fry, bar-b-que, or dinner) of supporters.

The campaign must establish clear and defensible ground rules to be followed for fundraising, such as, only designated supporters can solicit funds; there are some persons whose money will not be accepted for the campaign, and you cannot be left alone in a room with certain persons. (This is to avoid any accusations of improper soliciting of campaign funds.)

Fundraising begins with you and your family and associates. You must contribute to the campaign. Your family members, friends, and business associates will give to the campaign because of their close relationship with you. Others such as civic associates, lobbyists, political action committees, political organizations, and voters will give to you because the campaign message is one they support, or they believe you can be helpful in furthering their agenda.

Fundraising is all about you. You cannot be afraid to ask for money. If you do not ask for money, then no money will be raised for the campaign.

The size of the campaign's war chest has a direct bearing on the campaign's budget. The goal of the campaign is the same whether it is a campaign with lots of money or a campaign with little or no money, and that goal is to get 50 percent plus one of the votes on Election Day. The candidate who spends the most money does not assure himself of victory on Election Day. It is not how much money is spent but the use of the money that influences the outcome of an election.

The best use of campaign money is to "target" voters. The campaign must "target" those voters who are most likely to vote for the candidate. Care should be taken to identify voters who have some commonality with you. And when identified, the campaign must spend extra time wooing these voters. Every effort must be made to let these voters know of your candidacy; every effort must be made to get these voters to vote for you on Election Day.

CHAPTER 18

The Candidate and the Budget

A campaign budget must be developed for the campaign. The purpose of developing a budget is to determine how best to spend money raised to run a winning campaign maximizing efforts to 1) make contacts in the community to gain name recognition for the candidate, 2) get the campaign message to the voters, and 3) get 50 percent plus one of the votes for the candidate on Election Day.

You and your steering committee should not mistake the notion that if the campaign is a grass roots campaign (campaign run solely by volunteers), then no money is needed to run the campaign. In every campaign, including grass roots campaigns, money is needed to purchase campaign material, such as yard signs, car bumper stickers, and campaign buttons and pens; money is needed to purchase media ads and postage.

CHAPTER 19

A Campaign Headquarters Is Needed

Is a campaign headquarters needed? This is a question that all candidates ask. If you have been successful in raising funds, reaching an answer is not difficult; the answer is "yes."

If the campaign has no money, or limited money, you may reach the answer "no," without weighing the pros and cons of having a campaign headquarters. Why is a campaign headquarters needed? A campaign headquarters is needed for several reasons. The campaign needs a place for you to meet advisors. The campaign needs a place for you to meet volunteers. The campaign needs a place for voters to go to meet you and to get literature about the campaign. The campaign needs a central location to warehouse campaign literature. The campaign needs a place for those supporting your candidacy to meet to talk about the campaign and to encourage each other to work for the campaign.

While a campaign can be run without a campaign headquarters, the better practice is to have a campaign headquarters.

There is one other reason to have a campaign headquarters. The voters may not take the campaign serious if there is no campaign headquarters. Voters may believe that a lack of a campaign headquarters means you have no money and no support; meaning, you cannot win the election. A voter wants to support a candidate that he believes will win; no voter wants to vote for a candidate the voter believes has no chance to win. To deliver the subtle message that you have sufficient support to win you will need a campaign headquarters; this subtle message may be needed to convince some voters to give you their votes.

With campaigns finding increased uses of the Internet, an argument may be made that instead of an actual (physical) headquarters of brick and mortar, the candidate may use a virtual headquarters housed on the Internet since the cost to house the headquarters on the Internet would be less than the cost to house the headquarters at a physical location, and the campaign headquarters will be open all day, every day, if a virtual headquarters is used. However, because there are still voters who prefer to see and touch things and to see people in person, there are people who have a need for the physical contact that the Internet cannot give, a physical location for the headquarters is needed. And also because the campaign needs a place to house campaign literature, a physical location is needed.

The campaign should have both, a virtual headquarters on the Internet and a brick and mortar headquarters. This is so because, by having both, you have the best chance to reach all voters.

CHAPTER **20**

The Candidate Must
Encourage Early Voting

While the count of the votes cast on Election Day is important, you must not forget there are votes cast before Election Day that makes up the total votes cast on Election Day. Those votes cast before Election Day must be targeted by the campaign.

Early votes are votes cast before Election Day. If a voter meets certain criteria, he may vote early. You must designate a campaign worker whose sole responsibility will be to identify voters who are eligible to vote early.

The campaign worker should educate voters of their right to vote early. Voters should be encouraged to vote during the "early voting period." It is important that you win the vote count for the "early voting period." The failure to win this vote count could adversely affect your goal of getting 50 percent plus one of the votes cast on Election Day.

CHAPTER **21**

Yes, Hire a Political Consultant

You will be bombarded by calls from those who will offer to be your "hired hands"; this will include political consultants and salespeople selling their political wares (campaign material, i.e., yard signs), television and radio time, billboards, web pages, and more. You will need to take care not to be fooled by those who are looking to make money from the campaign.

You and members of the steering committee must decide what is needed for you to win. You and members of the steering committee must remember when deciding to spend money that a campaign plan has been crafted and careful thought was put into making decisions crafting the plan; no salesperson should change the course crafted for the campaign without a thorough discussion of whether the change being suggested by the salesperson will positively affect the campaign. Spending money is needed to get name recognition for the candidate, to get the vote out, and to secure the 50 percent plus one of the votes cast on Election Day. If the purchase being suggested by a salesperson does not help with the needs of the campaign within the budget of the campaign, the purchase should not be made.

You need a political consultant. Whether or not this will be a hired hand depends on whether there is money in the budget to pay a political consultant. If there is money to hire a political consultant, it will be money well spent to hire a political consultant. A good political consultant can 1) help with organizing the campaign; 2) assist with making decisions on how to raise money needed for the campaign; 3) help make critical decisions about campaign strategy; and 4) help make critical decisions on spending campaign dollars. While the final decision on any campaign question is to be made by you, it is helpful for you to have the input from one who has political knowledge and experience gained from being involved in other campaigns.

A political consultant will provide helpful information to identify what workers are needed to run the campaign. And the political consultant will be able to state what skills a person must have to fill a position of leadership in the campaign. This information will be helpful to determine what workers are needed and to identify who should hold leadership positions in the campaign.

A political consultant should be a source of knowledge when deciding what action you should take to get name recognition. Of particular concern in a campaign is "timing," the point in time a course of action should be taken by you. The political consultant using knowledge acquired in prior campaigns can help you to make the right decision at the right time.

The political consultant will know, from participating in prior elections, persons who donate to political campaigns; the political consultant can help you to identify these persons and can help you to get needed campaign dollars from those identified as potential campaign donors.

The key to determining whether a campaign has enough money to win an election is not how much money the campaign has to spend; it is how the money is spent. A political consultant should have ideas about the use of campaign dollars. The political consultant should be able to suggest, based on the circumstances of the campaign, where money should be spent to get the best results for the money spent.

CHAPTER 22

Yes, Maintain a Web Page

The campaign must have a web page. The web page should be designed to:

1. provide information about the candidate;
2. provide notice of upcoming events about the campaign;
3. solicit and communicate with campaign workers for the campaign; and
4. solicit and accept campaign donations.

And, as a part of the campaign, you must use all technological means of communicating to the voters; this includes using the web page and Facebook, tweeting, and using text messages and e-mails.

The campaign must designate a person to maintain the web page, and the web page must be updated daily. Only current information concerning the campaign should be made available on the web page to the public. Any information on the web page must be correct. And the web page must be user friendly; this is particularly so as it relates to the soliciting and acceptance of campaign contributions.

The web page is the campaign's virtual headquarters. You must walk through the virtual headquarters looking at the web page daily to insure only the message you approve has been placed on the web page. You must note what you see. You are responsible for the content of the web page, and because you are responsible, you must know what information the campaign is making available by way of the Internet to the public.

Because the web page is a campaign headquarters, you can be in the campaign headquarters each day. You can schedule office hours, allowing time for the voters to talk with you by way of the Internet.

CHAPTER **23**

Yes, Buy Newspaper Ads and, Radio and Television Ads

The campaign must get name recognition for your candidacy by getting the campaign message to the voters, and getting your story in the conscious of the voters. While going door-to-door, handing out campaign material is effective to get name recognition, because the geographic size of a political district may be large, you may not be able to cover the political district, going door-to-door. You must find other ways to contact the voters. The campaign must buy newspaper ads, radio and television ads to reach the voters.

When purchasing newspaper ads and radio and television ads, the campaign must target voters. The purpose of running any ad (newspaper, radio or television) is to reach voters; campaign money is not being spent to just say the campaign purchased an ad. The ad is run to get name recognition for your candidacy and to get the campaign message to the voters and to get your story in conscious of the voters, to get the voters to cast their ballots for you on Election Day.

You must hire professionals to design newspaper ads and to produce radio and television ads (spots). A good ad will get the attention of voters, resulting in a positive response from the voters. A poorly designed or worded ad will not be effective in getting a positive response from voters; in fact, it will likely get a negative response, losing votes for you. The campaign is more likely to get a good ad using the services of a professional; thus the reason to obtain the services of a professional, a person knowledgeable about writing and producing political ads.

An ad run must run more than one time to be effective to get noticed by the voters. The frequency of the number of times an ad is run on radio or television should increase as Election Day is approached, with the ad being run the greatest number of times on Election Day.

CHAPTER **24**

The Candidate Must Finish Election Day

You must work the campaign through the end of Election Day. Because you are the candidate, your supporters will look to you for directions for the campaign. If you relax before Election Day, your supporters will follow your lead, and they will relax. You must remind your supporters that campaigning must continue until all polling places are closed on Election Day. And you must demonstrate the urgency of the need to campaign through Election Day by working through Election Day.

You should not leave any votes at home on Election Day. You and your supporters must take action to get voters to their polling places on Election Day. You and your supporters must contact voters by telephone, and by going door-to-door, to encourage voters to vote on Election Day. You and your supporters must be visible in the voting district on Election Day, meeting voters, urging voters to go to the poll(s) and vote for you.

Chapter 25

The Candidate Ends the Campaign

After beginning the campaign, sometimes you may ask the question, why am I doing this? And, after asking this question, you begin the process of determining whether to continue running the campaign. If you have any doubts about whether the campaign should be continued, you must end the campaign.

There are reasons for ending a campaign prematurely. If the campaign is unable to raise the money necessary to pay the bills of the campaign, the campaign must be ended.

Another reason for ending a campaign is, if the key positions within the campaign cannot be filled and not having those positions filled is adversely affecting the running of the campaign. The campaign requires the efforts of more individuals than just the candidate.

You cannot run a campaign without the help of others. And, if there are no others who are willing to help you with your campaign, the campaign must be ended.

If any circumstance of the campaign has made it impossible for you to get your message to the voters, the campaign must be ended. For example, if the campaign involves a question that dominates the campaign, causing the campaign to be about you answering the question repeatedly (This usually happens when a "whisper campaign" about a possible misstep of the candidate has been initiated by someone sparking rumors and smearing the candidate's name.), making it impossible for you to get your message to the voters, then the campaign must be ended.

Sometimes, the campaign must be ended because the candidate realizes that running was not his idea, it was the idea of another. The candidate is running because he was told by another that he would be a good candidate. And, after beginning the campaign, the candidate learns that it is "hard work and costly" to run a campaign. The candidate decides the cost to run is too great; he does not want to devote what is required of his time, talents, and treasures to run a campaign.

Just like the decision to run a campaign is one to be made by the candidate, the decision to end a campaign is one to be made by the candidate. This is not to say the candidate does not need to consult with others to make the decision to end a campaign; the candidate should and must consider the counsel of others; the steering committee and close family members must be consulted. While the candidate must listen and consider the counsel of others, the final decision to continue the campaign is a decision that the candidate must make and the final decision to end a campaign is a decision that the candidate must make.

If you decide to end the campaign, you must first tell your family of the decision. And, after doing so, you must personally inform your steering committee and close supporters of the decision. A public announcement, ending the campaign must be made. The reason for ending a campaign does not have to be made public; you need only to say, "I am ending my campaign." And when ending a campaign prematurely, you must not forget to thank your supporters publicly and privately.

CHAPTER **26**

The Candidate as a Newly Elected Official

After running a campaign resulting in you being elected to office, you are now that "somebody that ought to do something." You are now the candidate-elect, you are empowered by the vote to "do something," and you must not be afraid to exercise the authority of the office; you must "do something."

In addition to "doing something," you must treat the office with care and respect. The office must not be abused or mistreated. "The office belongs to the people and not to a select few who has an agenda that is self-serving." You must never forget that it is the people's office, and "the vote of the office" must be used to promote the general welfare of the people who put you in office.

PART II

Thoughts of an Elected Official

No experience you have will adequately prepare you for a term as an elected official. Neither your education nor your work experience can adequately prepare you for being an elected official.

Part II gives the reader—particularly those who aspire to be an elected official—an insight into being an elected official. It is not all of what you need to know about being an elected official. But it provides critical observations that must not be ignored, particularly the observation that being elected to office will change you. The change can be for "better" or "worst." And, only the elected official can decide whether the office will change him/her for "better" or "worst."

CHAPTER **27**

Day after the Election

The campaign has been completed and you have won; you are now an elected official. Your supporters are happy, your family is happy, and you are happy. What is your first task as a newly elected official? You must thank all persons who worked tirelessly in the campaign; without your supporters and workers, you would not have won the election.

There are individuals that must be told "thank-you" in person. This includes members of the steering committee and family members. Others may be told "thank-you" by telephone calls, written notes, texts, or e-mails. It is important to thank those who helped you, because you will need their help to run your office (and for any future campaigns).

The day after the election, you need to rest. The campaign has been long and difficult, and you have devoted countless hours to the campaign. You need to rest your mind and body.

You must take time to reflect and think about what it means for you to be an elected official. You are a servant occupying a position of trust.

You must not forget that you occupy a position of trust given to you by the voters. The position you occupy belongs to the people. You are only the steward; you do not own the office. At all times, you must remember to use the position to carry out the people's business in a fair and just manner, and you must use the position to promote the general welfare of the people.

CHAPTER **28**

A Review of the Campaign and the People Who Help

Following the election, you must review the campaign. You must critically review all facets of the campaign, namely 1) action taken to gain name recognition; 2) action taken to get the vote out through the communication efforts of the campaign; 3) action taken to raise money; 4) action taken to get the vote during the early voting period; 5) action taken to get the voters to the polls to vote on Election Day; and 6) action taken to finish the campaign on Election Day. The steering committee must be encouraged to discuss the good and the bad of the campaign. And, observations about the campaign must be made to insure future campaigns will be run better than the last campaign.

You should evaluate the people who helped in the campaign. Those persons who brought marketable skills to the campaign and who did a good job should be considered for employment, when possible, to fill positions to help you run the office that you now occupy.

If these persons were good enough to run and win an election, then they (where possible) are good enough to fill positions of the office to help you carry out the responsibilities of your office. Even if your close advisors are not a part of the office workforce, you should keep in contact with the close advisors during your term in office; their counsel may prove to be valuable for you when you are faced with difficult situations requiring a decision, just as their counsel was for you during the campaign.

CHAPTER **29**

What Do the Voters Want?

After taking the oath of office, your attention will immediately turn to answering the question, "What do the voters want me to do?" Are the voters only concerned about the "single issue" you were elected to answer on their behalf as a member of the governing body, or do the voters want you to be the representative not only for them but for all the people?

Not only must you quickly decide what the voters want, but you must also develop a relationship with the voters. The voters must believe you are "approachable." The voters must believe that they can come to you, and if a cause or concern of the community is brought to you, you will honestly make the cause or concern your cause or concern. And, you will work tirelessly toward the end of ensuring the community causes and/or concerns brought to you are favorably dealt with by you and the "body politics."

You must continue to cultivate your relationship with the voters. You, the elected official, must become and be the voice of the community you represent in the "body politics."

In your role as the community voice, you must be "reasoned" in your advocacy. Just as you must support the cause or concern of the community, you must be strong enough to say "no," to the community when you are asked to voice a cause or concern that you know is not in the best interest of all of the people. You must be willing to "educate" the voters of the "true needs" of the community based on your study of the community and its needs, and you must have courage to do what is right for all the people.

As an elected official, you must remain in contact with the voters and the community you represent. You should be present at community meetings, and when necessary, you must schedule community meetings to keep the community informed of actions needed for the betterment of all.

You should use print, radio and television media, and the Internet to stay in communication with the voters. You should have, and maintain, a web page.

And, you must respond to letters and telephone calls from the voters and others. Too often, elected officials fail and/or refuse to answer communications addressed to them—particularly those communications that are critical of action taken. A response must be given. You do not want the voters to say you do not care about your community. If you are not seen in the community; and if the voters do not hear from you, the voters will have a factual basis for the belief you do not care about them. This is so, even though you may be doing a good job in the body politics representing your community.

CHAPTER **30**

Consequences of Being Elected

After the election, you will notice that there will be those who will think you have become smarter; they will consider you to be an expert on matters that you know very little about. Because people believe you are now an expert, they will invite you to speak in their organizations and clubs. Everybody will want to know your opinion on matters of concern (to them), and when you speak, people will listen because now you are an expert.

You will find that "not only have you become smarter" but also that your jokes will garner laughter. You will tell the very same jokes told in the past that got no laughter; but when these jokes come out of the mouth of the candidate-elect, the jokes will be funny and people will laugh.

While you have become smarter to some, others will find you to be another dumb politician. There will be those who will question your answer to every question. These will be the people who will ask, "How did such a dumb person get elected to office?" The consequence of being elected is that they will criticize all that you say. And there will be those who will find all that you do to be "just plain stupid."

By occupying the office, you now have the power of the office; people expect you to use the office power fighting for their causes. If you do, you are smart; if you do not, you are dumb.

The truth is you have not become smarter or dumber. You are the same person who you were before you were elected to office.

What has changed is you are now the government representative in the community; now you are responsible for all matters of concern of the community. And you are responsible to all persons living in the community.

Because you are now the government in your community, you must strive to be fair and just in your decision-making. It is through your efforts that government will be fair and just. By your actions (and your votes in the body politics), you must insure that the government is responsive and responsible to the needs and wants of all citizens in the community. Government is for those who disagree with you too; you must not forget that government is for them too. You must never forget government is for all the people.

As an elected official, you are no longer a community organizer, one who is only concerned about a single cause; you are now the government representative in your community. You have the responsibility to advocate for all causes to support the positive growth of the entire community.

As an elected official, you represent the government's presence in your community. This means when your community speaks about the government action or inaction, the community is talking about you, the elected official.

You, as an elected official, must be concerned about the general welfare of the entire community, and any action you take must demonstrate a concern for the general welfare of the entire community.

CHAPTER **31**

The Elected Official and the Lobbyist

One of the first persons you will meet after being elected to office is a lobbyist, a person hired to advocate for a specific cause, a specific entity, or a specific person. The lobbyist will have information and facts and figures to show you how just and right the lobbyist's cause is. The lobbyist will present himself to be a treasure trove of knowledge on matters that he is asking you to support.

The lobbyist will present himself as a friend. The lobbyist will do whatever it takes to feed your ego, in order to make you believe that you are more than just an elected official to him and that you are his best friend. The lobbyist will make a financial contribution to your campaign. The lobbyist will pay for your breakfast, lunch, and dinner. The lobbyist will purchase tickets for you to attend concerts, sporting events, and other gala affairs. The lobbyist will also "ghost" write and publish articles for you so you can demonstrate "your" knowledge on important matters casting you as an expert on the matters. Of course, the matter just happens to be the cause the lobbyist is supporting.

Why does the lobbyist spend time and money on you? It is all about the vote you have, based on you being an elected official. The lobbyist is developing a relationship with you so that he will feel comfortable asking you to vote in support of his cause, and the lobbyist believes if he has a friendship with you, you will support his cause.

As an elected official, you must be careful not to become so close to a lobbyist that you forget why you ran for public office. You ran for public office because you were concerned about the general welfare of those persons living in your community; you did not run for office to be the spokesperson for a select few, for a special interest group represented by the lobbyist.

The lobbyist should be a source of information that you gather with other information to decide how best to vote on a matter being considered by the body politics. The lobbyist should not be the only source of information. As always, your vote should be guided by principles of fairness and justice; you are forever seeking what is good for your community.

CHAPTER **32**

It's Just Politics

Often you as an elected official will hear the words, "It is nothing personal, it's just politics." In the beginning, it will be difficult for you to not hear, "It is personal," when these words are spoken. Usually, these words ("It is nothing personal, it's just politics.") are spoken by a fellow member of the governing body to you to justify that person's failure to be supportive of you after promising to support you.

You have legislation that needs one more vote to pass to be accepted by the governing body. A fellow member of the governing body has agreed to be that vote you need. Your matter is brought before the body for a vote. Your fellow member votes but not in support of your matter; he votes against your matter.

And when you confront the fellow member, challenging his vote, he responds, "It is nothing personal, it's just politics."

This will not be the last time a fellow member disappoints you with a vote. While it may be difficult not to accept the disappointment as personal, your time as an elected official will be best served by not taking any disappointing vote(s) personal. Most people who are elected to public office are honorable men and women. And, those persons elected to public office want to do what is right. Just like you, they have the responsibility of engaging in the mental gymnastics of balancing competing interests and when doing so, what is right is not always easily determined. In fact, you will learn that the right answer is relative in a lot of situations.

CHAPTER **33**

Politics Is the Art of Compromise

You will hear the phrase, "Politics is the art of compromise." You should be careful to take time to understand what is meant by this phrase. This phrase does not mean you should abandon your position(s) on a matter to go along with what another is suggesting to be the right way of doing something.

And it does not mean that when you take a position on a matter, you are so tied to your position until your position becomes more important than the matter before the governing body. You should not allow your position to overshadow your responsibility to govern. If you do, then you will lose your focus on providing for the general welfare of the people who are subject to the actions of the governing body.

Is politics the art of compromise? It is; when governing, those who are elected to office must find a way to keep the government running and avoid a shutdown of the government. You and the other members of the body politics are responsible for the well-being of people. You cannot carry out this responsibility if the government shuts down. To keep the government running, you may have to compromise your position to keep the government running.

When saying politics is the art of compromise, this simply means you cannot get all that you want all the time; there will be times you will need to change your position and keep the government running. However, when doing this, you must work to insure that the business of government will be done without anyone, or any group being unfairly hurt. At all times, you as an elected official must be careful when running the government to insure no person or group is unfairly burdened by any action of the government. You must insist that the principles of fairness and justice be a part of any compromise reached.

Chapter 34

Money and Politics

Another phrase you will hear repeatedly during your term in office is, "Politics is a game that rich people play."

When surveying the political landscape, considering those who are elected to office and the costs associated with running a campaign, you will conclude "money" plays a role in an election. And considering the time you and your colleagues spend on the government budget, you will conclude "money" plays a role in governing.

A candidate for public office must have money to pay for the campaign; campaign literature must be purchased; use of the print, radio and television media cost money; there is travel costs associated with moving about the voting district; to house the campaign, a campaign headquarters is needed at a cost to the campaign. And, because there is a finite amount of money to be spent, the candidate must decide how best to spend money raised for the campaign.

And, after being elected to office, the elected official will spend time raising money to pay for the next campaign.

The elected official also spends time trying to decide how best to spend the people's money, tax dollars, when crafting a budget for the government. There are programs to fund to promote the general welfare of the people; there are programs to fund to provide for the public safety and health of the people; there are programs to fund to provide for the education of the people. And, there are projects in your community needing money to promote the general welfare of the people.

And, because there is a finite amount of money to be spent, you must decide how best to spend the people's money.

Perhaps, instead of saying "politics is a game that rich people play," what should be said is both the candidate and the elected official will spend time determining how best to spend money.

CHAPTER **35**

The Elected Official Must Use the Power of the Office

The power of the elected official depends largely upon 1) his ability to put money in the budget for his community; and 2) his ability to influence the action(s) of the body politics to effect change in his community.

The voters want to see a government presence in their community. The voters measure government presence by the amount of money that the government spends in the community that the voters call "home." You must work to put money in the budget to be spent in your community. And, you must work to insure the amount of money spent in your community is fair; it must be more than a token. It must be an amount that is serious enough to make a difference in the community.

You must develop relationships with other members of the body politics that will allow you to pass legislation needed to address the concerns of the voters and other members of your community. And, if you cannot get legislation passed, you must, through relationships, position yourself to influence legislation that will make a positive difference in your community. You must have the courage to make known to the body politics the needs of your community. And, you must have the "know-how" to get the work done in the body politics that will positively address the concerns in the community you represent.

CHAPTER **36**

Should a Cause Be Law?

You began your term in office with a mandate to support the causes you championed while campaigning. You began your service by stating with certainty the causes you support. You soon learn that those who serve with you have causes they support, and their causes sometimes are in direct opposition to your causes. You learn that to get your causes supported by others, you must be willing to change your opinion on causes you thought you opposed; change your causes "slightly" to get support needed for the causes; and you must be willing to accept an extended timetable for making your causes the law. In short, you learn that politics is the art of compromise.

Soon you begin to wonder whether you will be able to keep promises made to the voters to make the causes of your campaign the law of the land. Voters begin to contact you, asking for an update on when you are going "to make good on your campaign promises."

Should a Cause Be Law?

As time passes, you learn that governing is not easy. You learn that some actions (even those supporting a good cause) can have unintended consequences that may have bad results for someone or some group of people, and not every cause should be law. You may conclude a cause should not be law. And when this decision is made, you must have the courage to tell the voters that the cause is a bad one, and it should not be law.

Just as you will learn that there are causes that should not be law, you will learn that there are causes that must be law. Some may not be popular, but yet justice and fairness demand that the causes be law. It is your responsibility to accept the challenge and take action to make these causes the law.

CHAPTER **37**

You Will Not Benefit Financially by Being in Office

Being an elected official will not bring to you monetary wealth. You will not experience any positive gain in monetary wealth while you are serving as an elected official; you may see a drop in your net worth after serving as an elected official. The federal government, most states, and local governments have laws against an elected official engaging in activity associated with his office that allows the elected official or his family members to benefit financially from any action associated with the office.

While you did not enter politics for financial gain, you should be careful not to allow your time as an elected official ruin you financially. You must be financially secure if you are going to be in office. If you lack money to adequately support your financial obligations, you will not be an effective elected official because concerns about your finance will dominate your time and attention, not the business of the office, affecting your ability to carry out your duties as an elected official.

CHAPTER **38**

You Must Define Who You Are

Prior to being elected to office, you will be labeled, and when you take office, you will be labeled. You are labeled by your political party affiliation, you are labeled by your statements on matters being considered by the body politics, you are labeled by your voting history, and you are labeled by who your political associates are.

The purpose of you being labeled is to answer the question, "Who are you?" and to predict how you will vote on matters coming before the body politics.

Most people will know very little about your personal history. They will not know what schools you attended, nor will they know what degrees you hold. Most people will not know your immediate family members, nor will they know your neighbors. But yet, these same people will claim to know you because of the labels that have been put on you.

Not only will people claim to know you by your labels, people involved in politics and your colleagues in the body politics will claim to know you by your voting record on political matters coming before the body politics. You will be labeled by your voting record.

There will be those who will support you; some will even contribute financially to your campaign because of your labels. And, there will be those who will oppose you because of your labels.

How you are viewed by the public by the labels you wear will determine what power and influence you will have in the body politics. If the members of the body politics believe you are favorably viewed by the public because of the labels you wear, you will be viewed as having the support of the public, which will give you power and influence in the body politics to get things done.

While what the public says about you, defining you, is important. It is more important that you answer the question, "Who am I?" You must define yourself.

You must through thoughtful and measured action define who you are; you must decide what labels you will wear, and by doing so, you will determine how you are viewed by the public.

You must answer the question, "Who am I?" before you seek to define yourself by the labels you wear. And, when answering the question, "Who am I?" you must do so honestly. If you fail to honestly answer this question, you will be, forever, seeking to find yourself in the comments of friends and foes. Not knowing who you are will allow others to answer the question for you by the labels they put on you. If this is done, when you hear public comments being made about you, you may not know the comments are referring to you, because you do not know who you are.

CHAPTER **39**

Use Time Wisely

As an elected official, you want to help anybody and everybody. You accept appointments and engagements; your calendar will be filled with events needing your time and attention. And, before long, you will be overwhelmed by the demands on your time.

You will begin to complain about there not being enough time in the day to complete scheduled tasks.

With your election to office, demands will be made on your time; it will seem everyone wants you to give your time to a cause. It will seem that if a person is not calling for an office appointment, someone is calling to invite you to an event or someone is calling to complain about your failure to be present for an event.

Care should be taken to not "overcommit" yourself to people and events. Being an elected official does not mean you must see everyone who comes to your office. Being an elected official does not mean you must attend every event that you are invited to attend. You need to determine what requires your personal attention and what does not. And, if something does not require your personal attention, it is acceptable to allow an aide to go in your place. In some cases, it is acceptable for an aide to meet with an individual or group of individuals in your place at your office. And in some cases it is okay to say "no" to an invitation.

If you do not wisely use your time, you will not have time to do the job you were elected to do. You were elected to attend to matters coming before the body politics. Attending to matters before the body politics requires time for you to study the matters and educate yourself on what is the best action to take on the matters. You need time to work with other elected officials on matters before the body politics. And, you must be present when action is taken on matters before the body politics.

It is important that you learn how to say "no." And you do not have to give a reason for your saying "no"; not all invites or requests for appointments require your attention.

If you do not learn to prioritize your time, and if you do not learn how to say "no," you will not have time for your family, nor will you have time for yourself.

It is important that you schedule "uninterrupted time" for your family. When spending time with your family, you must be present, both physically and mentally. You should never schedule a "working family vacation"; if you do so, you will invariably find yourself working and not vacationing and enjoying time with your family.

You must find time for yourself. Your body and mind need rest. You need time to think. You need time away from everyone, including family members and friends. Find the time alone that you need. Only you know how much alone time you need. Find the time, use it wisely; use the time to think, reflect, and relax.

CHAPTER **40**

To Effect Change,
Show up for Meetings

If you are elected to office, you must be present when the body politics meets. The voters put you in office to be their voice in the body politics. You cannot carry out the voters' wishes if you are not present for meetings scheduled to do the work of the body politics.

Even if you disagree with the action of the body politics, you must be present to state why you oppose the action to be taken. Not only should you state why you oppose the proposed action, you should have an alternative for the body politics to consider, and you must argue to gain support for your alternative.

Even if you believe you will lose the argument to support or oppose a matter before the body politics, you must be present to argue your position, being respectful of others at all times. Governing is not personal; it is about issues and ideas and about how best to provide for the general welfare of the people being governed.

If you are present for the vote of the body politics on an action to be taken, you have an opportunity to change the minds of your fellow elected officials and just maybe you will change the mind of the one person that will make the difference needed to change the vote to get the outcome you wish to obtain.

By failing to show up, you guarantee that which you want done for the voters will not be done because you were not present for the vote of the body politics. By failing to show up, you have failed the voters who put you in office on the promise to be present to vote on matters coming before the body politics. By failing to show up, you have abdicated your responsibility to govern. You cannot govern if you are not present when the body politics meets.

You cannot effect change if you are not present in the body politics to argue for change. If you want to have change, you must be present and argue for change before a vote is taken by the body politics.

In most situations, your failure to show up will not stop the body politics from taking action (even if your presence is needed for a quorum for the body politics to take official action, the body politics can meet and take unofficial action without a quorum). Your choices are to be present and vote or to be absent and let your colleagues vote for you.

If you are elected to office, show up for meetings, voice your opinions, advocate for your constituents, and vote. Being absent from a meeting, will not force your colleagues to vote for your position on any matter. Being absent from a meeting will not stop the body politics from taking action.

CHAPTER **41**

Be a Statesperson

Once you take office, you should remember that your responsibility includes more than just being one who oppose actions of the body politics. This is not to say you should not oppose those actions you believe, if made the law, will not to be in the best interest of the people. When the body politics threaten to take or actually take action that is harmful, action that will unfairly burden or hurt any group of people governed, then it is your duty to be vocal in your opposition to the unfair or unjust action of the body politics.

If possible, it is your responsibility to offer an alternative to the action of the body politics. No one person has a monopoly on the brain trust on any ideas. There will always be alternatives to any proposed action of the body politics. If you have an alternative that you deem to be the best action to be taken by the body politics, then you must offer your alternative to the body politics for consideration and vote.

To insure that you are prepared to make a good decision on matters coming before the body politics, you must seek knowledge to help you understand that which is before you. You must study the matter; this includes using the information of experts to help you understand the matter. And, when making a decision to support, or not to support a matter, you must show wisdom; this includes supporting the best interest of those governed even when some voters oppose the action you are supporting. Knowledge and wisdom are the keys to insuring you make the best decision concerning matters coming before the body politics.

CHAPTER **42**

Respect Your Colleagues

After you are elected to office, it is important that you and your fellow elected officials respect each other. You will have philosophical differences; you must argue for your point of view. You and your fellow elected officials have constituents, those voters who put you in office and who expect for you to be their advocate in the body politics. You must advocate on behalf of your constituents, and your fellow elected officials must advocate on behalf of their constituents. All this may lead to a difference of opinion as to what should be the will of the body politics. This difference of opinion should not lead to personal bickering between you and your fellow elected officials; you must remember that you were elected to promote the general welfare of those whom you were elected to govern and not to fight with a fellow elected official because you don't like the person. Neither you nor any fellow elected official have a monopoly on the answer to the questions coming before the body politics. In order for the body politics to function properly, it is important that all elected officials respect the opinions of others and be respectful to each other.

This does not mean you cannot disagree with other elected officials. You can disagree with your fellow elected officials, and you can be vocal, stating why you disagree. However, you must not be disagreeable, quarrelsome in voicing your difference of opinion.

Further, you should not make personal attacks against any fellow elected official, even one who you may have a disagreement with. When voicing your difference of opinion, you should debate the question being discussed by the body politics and not whether you like your fellow elected official.

You should not shy away from fairly and vigorously debating matters being considered by the body politics for fear of causing tension in the body politics. This is so as long as you are searching for the truth to insure that whatever decision reached by the body politics is best for all persons being governed. You should never argue just for the sake of arguing.

And, when possible, you should support your fellow elected officials. Not all matters need to be argued, and not all matters need to be opposed by you. If you develop a reputation of being an obstructionist, arguing and opposing all matters, don't be surprised when you ask for support on a matter (you can do nothing in the body politics without the help of your fellow elected officials), your fellow elected officials will not give you any support.

CHAPTER **43**

Did I Do a Good Job?

Probably the most difficult assessment to be made after a term in office is answering the question, "What kind of job did I do?" This cannot be answered until you first determine why you should be returned to office by the voters?

When determining "Why you should be returned to office as an elected official?" A number of other questions should come to mind, and they are as follows:

1. Do I truly understand what is at stake for an elected official and what are the needs of the community I represent?
2. Do I really represent the community? What do the community and I have in common?
3. Were the campaign and the time in office about ideas? If so, then whose ideas were represented by the campaign and the term in office?
4. Is anyone inspired to do "good" by my efforts to govern?

If you understand the needs of the community, and you, through your ideas, addressed the needs, inspiring others to see the needs and help with addressing the needs, then the voters should return you to office. And you can say with certainty you did a good job.

CHAPTER 44

Do I Want to Do This Again?

Your term in office is drawing to an end; you are reflecting on your time in office. It seems like it was just yesterday you were taking the oath of office. You wonder where the time has gone.

You remember the first constituent who visited you to thank you for a vote made by you that brought help to him. You remember the first lunch you had with a lobbyist. You remember your first victory on the floor of the governing body. You remember all the good you did helping others. And, you remember the defeats of your term in office.

The term in office was more difficult than you imagined it would be; sure you knew you would have to work to get things done, but you never thought every effort to get anything done would be met with opposition.

You got to know all too well the saying, "Public service requires sacrifice." You missed birthday parties because your presence was needed at political events. Family time was always taking a backseat to politics. Your family members have commented that politics has taken their place.

You look at your bank account, and it has been reduced in size because of the financial demands placed upon you by your office. You had to use your personal fund to meet the demands of your office; public money was not always available to reimburse you for political expenditures.

As you continue to reflect on your time in office, you began to ask yourself, "Do I want to do this again? Do I want to serve another term in office?"

And, the deciding factor whether to run for another term is whether you can balance the demands of the office, with the needs of your family, and your desire for private time. If you are not able to balance the demands of the office with the needs of your family, you could lose the future election, and worst, you could lose your family. If you are not able to balance the demands of the office with your desire for private time, you could lose your sanity. Only you can decide whether you can perform the balancing of demands, needs, and desires that you know must be balanced. If there is any doubt as to whether you can balance the demands, needs, and desires, then you should not run for another term in office.

CHAPTER **45**

It Is Time to Quit

There is a beginning, and there is an end to all matters. You entered politics the day you accepted the challenge to be "somebody" to take a community need to the body politics for corrective action. You remember the excitement of being elected and saying to your community, "Thank you for allowing me to be your representative to the body politics." And, you remember also, the anxious feeling you had because of the uncertainty of what lay ahead for you and for your community. You did not know whether the community would accept your service. You did not know whether you could get the body politics to see the need of your community, and you did not know whether you could get the body politics to act in a responsible way to help your community.

While the time of beginning is certain, the ending time is uncertain. When is it "quitting time?" When should you decide "I have served, and it is now time for me to end my time as a public servant."?

You should quit if you decide you just don't like the job. There is nothing wrong with not liking the job responsibilities of an elected official. And, if you don't want to perform the job duties, then you should "quit."

You should quit if you believe you are no longer effective in the position that you occupy. An elected official has power and influence that is tied to the office. Any person holding the office is the "holder of the *power* and *influence*" that go with the office. If you are afraid to use the power and/or influence of the office, or if you believe you cannot effectively use the power and/or influence of the office to effect the change needed to help your community, then you need to quit.

If you believe you can better serve your community by using your talents, not as an elected official but as a community advocate, then you should quit.

The office belongs to the people; if at any time you begin to think "the office belongs to you," you should quit.

And finally, if you cannot balance the demands of the office with the needs of your family and your desire to have some private time, then you should quit.

CHAPTER **46**

A Term in Office Will Change You

After serving a term as an elected official, it would not be unusual for you to hear whispers of complaint about who you have become. And it would not be unusual for those closest to you to say, "I don't know you anymore, who are you?" You look the same as you did before being elected to office, and your voice sounds the same as it did before you were elected to office, but yet, you are being told that you are not the same person you were before being elected to office.

Has your time in office changed you? The time in office will change you.

You may be changed by the trappings, exaggerated attention and adulation given to you by those who seek the power and influence of the office if you believe you are better than others because of what is being said about you. People will tell you how great you are; some will say you are an expert on matters you may know nothing about.

People will say you possess great wit with humor; some will laugh at your sayings, including your bad jokes.

There will be those who will want to be in your presence simply because you are an elected official. You will be invited to attend functions back home, and there will be occasions when you are asked to speak to those gathered at the function because you have words of wisdom to share with others simply because you are an elected official.

You may be changed by the teachings of the body politics; the body politics is a classroom, the teachers are those senior members of the body politics that have knowledge based on years of experience, and you, the junior member, have the privilege to acquire knowledge from the senior members. The knowledge you acquire by your participation in the body politics may change you.

After a term in office, you should become a stronger and "better" advocate for the people and causes that sent you to the body politics because of the knowledge you have acquired from being a member of the body politics. After a term in office, you should have the courage, conviction, and consciousness to do what is right because of the knowledge you have acquired from being a member of the body politics.

You must work not to allow the trappings of the office to change you for the "worst" causing you to think you are better than others and you are entitled to the exaggeration adulation that is being given to you. You should listen to what is being said by close family members and friends who worked to put you in office; if they say you have changed, make sure they are not saying the change is for the "worst."

You want your time in office to change you for the "better." You want to use the knowledge and experience you have acquired, coupled with the power and influence of the office, to make life "better" for those you represent.

CHAPTER **47**

A Concluding Thought about Change

Serving in an elected office will change you. The body politics and those you meet will educate you about politics, and with this education, you will complete your term in office as a more knowledgeable person of political affairs than the person who was elected to office. Additionally, the trappings, i.e., being catered to by all you meet by being told you are so important, will change you. The knowledge acquired and/or the trappings of the office will change you; the question is, will you be changed for the "better" or for the "worst?"

How will others view your time in office? Will those who know you consider you to be a servant of the community or one who wish to be served by the community? Whether you are seen as a servant or one who wish to be served will be determinative of whether you have been changed for the "better" or for the "worst." If you now want to be served, you have changed for the "worst." If you want to be of service to others, you have changed for the "better."

You must be careful not to allow the office to change you for the "worst." You must not forget that you were sent to the body politics to serve your community and others, and not to be served.

EPILOGUE

Campaigning is demanding. If you want to be an elected official, you must commit yourself totally to the campaign. You must give your time, talent and treasure to the campaign. There are no short cuts to running a campaign.

As the candidate you are the face of the campaign. All eyes will be focus on you. Whether you receive the support of others will depend on how you are viewed by those who are watching you. And, you will get a vote only if you are viewed as being an advocate for the cause that is most important to the voter.

Campaigning is all about the candidate. And because you are the candidate, during the campaign the voters will desire your presence. It is you that the voters want.

If you are able to win your election, soon thereafter upon taking the oath of office you (as the candidate-elect) will learn that there has been a subtle shift in the desire of the voters. You will learn that it is the office that you have by way of the election, which will be the target of the desire of the voters. It is no longer you that is important to the voters, but it is the office that will be desired by the voters.

After being elected to office, you must be careful not to be confused by this subtle shift in the desire of the voters. If you are not careful you will continue to believe it is still all about you as it was during the campaign and you will act and believe you are more important than the office. You must respect the office and the power that comes with the office. You must exercise the power of the office for the people. You must be careful that you do not become drunk by the power of the office and in a drunken stupor began to demand that you be served and you forget to serve the people.

You must never forget that your run for office was based on your wish to be that somebody to do something for the general welfare of the people. And you must use the power of the office to serve the people; you must never use the power of the office to serve yourself.

APPENDICES

Part I

The Campaign Is All about the Candidate

Appendix A

The Candidate's To-Do List

Before making a public announcement, the candidate must do the following:

- Discuss candidacy with family and friends
- Name political consultant
- Name a campaign chairperson and treasurer
- Name a legal advisor
- Gather information about election laws
- Begin fundraising by asking family and friends for financial support
- Open campaign bank account for campaign
- Create web page; name person who will be responsible for updating web page

- Meet with steering committee members and delegate responsibilities of campaign
- Gather supporters on _____*(date)* for initial meeting of steering committee

After making an announcement, the candidate must do the following:

- Open campaign headquarters on _____*(date)*
- Name an office manager(s) on _____*(date)*
- Communicate with potential supporters
- Develop timeline for the campaign
- Craft a campaign slogan
- Designate campaign color(s)
- Design literature for the campaign
- Draft campaign message
- Prepare news kit

The candidate must do the following to create name recognition:

- Target key individuals and organizations to obtain "endorsements"
- Name campaign spokesperson for communication to media

The candidate must do the following to raise money:

- Establish place, date, and time for fundraiser(s)

The candidate must do the following to get votes:

- Recruit volunteers
- Canvass in the neighborhood, beginning _____*(date)*
- Do first mail-out/target actual voters
- Develop radio and television spots
- Put out yard signs, beginning _____*(date)*
- Put out billboard, beginning _____*(date)*
- Run radio ads, beginning _____*(date)*
- Run television ads, beginning _____*(date)*

- Target early voters, beginning _____ *(date)*
- Target absentee voters, beginning _____ *(date)*

The candidate must do the following to be prepared for Election Day:

- Prepare for Election Day by developing an action plan to be followed on Election Day by the steering committee
- The candidate must not forget to vote on Election Day
- The action plan developed must be implemented on Election Day

Appendix B

Eight things to know about steering committee meetings

The following points must be considered each time the steering committee meets:

1. Have an agenda and follow the agenda.
2. Review a one-page report (minutes) of last meeting.
3. Meet for only one hour.
4. Be passionate about the campaign.
5. Be mindful of *campaign timeline.*
6. Remember the steering committee meets to devise campaign strategies for getting votes; it does not meet for those present to tell war stories.
7. A person other than the candidate should chair the meeting.
8. Prior to the meeting, the candidate must meet with chairperson and person chairing the meeting to prepare for the meeting.

Appendix C

Campaign Timeline

Event(s)	Date
Election Day	
Early Voting Registration	
Absentee Balloting Begins	
Television Ads Begin	
Radio Ads Begin	
Billboards Begin	
Newspaper/Print Media Begin	
Fundraising Event (last)	
Foot Canvassing Begin	
Fundraising Event (first)	
Mail-out Begin/E-mailing	
Identify Workers/Volunteers	
Announcement Web page	
Meet with Steering Committee Organizational structure	

Appendix D

Campaign Organizational Chart

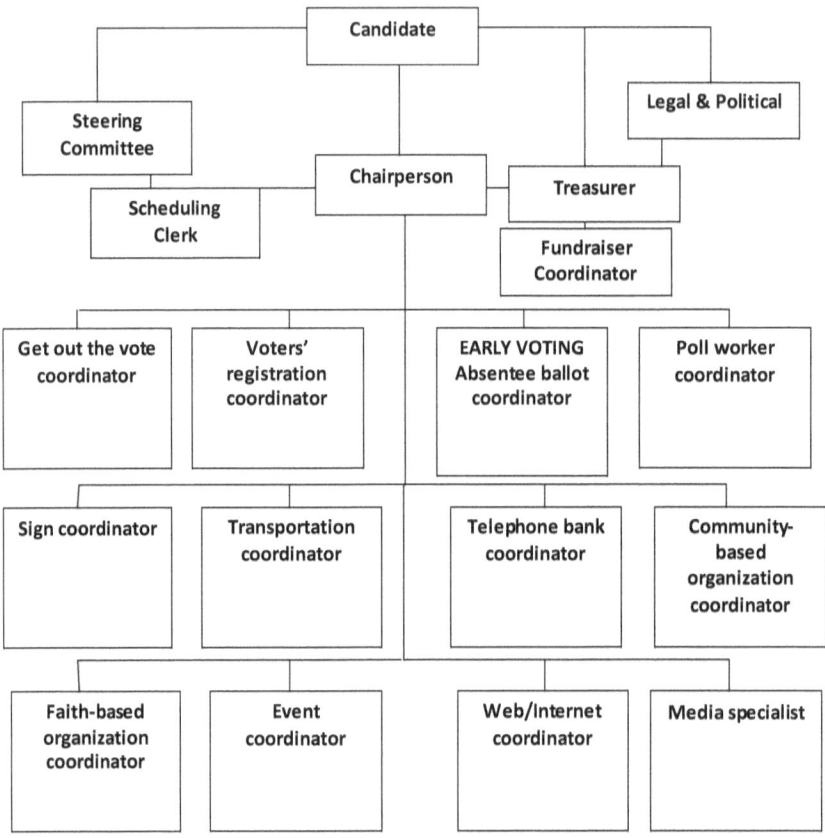

Appendix E

Glossary

actual voter. A person whose voting history shows that he votes in every election cycle.

campaign platform. A statement developed by the candidate showing his position on the issues of the campaign.

campaign spokesperson. The person who is responsible for insuring the candidate's message is made available to the media, print, radio, television, and Internet. This person is responsible for monitoring news in the media concerning the campaign; of particular concern to be monitored are stories about the candidate. This person manages the news being put in the public domain by the campaign about the candidate.

campaign timeline. A calendar showing the key dates and events in the life of the campaign, which must be followed by the campaign. It tells the candidate where the campaign is and where the campaign is headed.

candidate's steering committee. Steering committee members are advisors who are the candidate's "inner circle." They are expected to provide information for the campaign. They are to continually look at the campaign, identifying strengths and weaknesses, helping the candidate to chart a course for the campaign. Steering committee members must believe in the campaign and the candidate, and each member must demonstrate that belief by action.

chairperson. The person who manages the campaign, assisting the candidate with completing the candidate's "To-Do" List, taking steps to insure that the campaign stays on timeline and communicating with the staff, both paid and volunteered, about the campaign. This person must remain passionate about the campaign and the candidate, encouraging the staff, both paid and volunteered, to work for the election of the candidate through the day of election.

grass roots campaign. A campaign that is run primarily by the candidate and his supporters going door-to-door, courting the voters in the community, and there is little money spent to contact voters. It is a campaign strategy used most often when there is very little money to be used for the campaign.

legal advisor. This person is responsible for insuring that the campaign does not run afoul of any local, state, or federal election laws.

political consultant. A political consultant is one who understands politics. A political consultant must help the candidate create an image and a message, and the political consultant must be aware of what is being said in the voting district. A political consultant must tell the truth. This is done not to kill an idea, but so that the best efforts can be taken to insure that an idea has the best chance to be a "positive" for the candidate.

political hot spot. A place located in the community where politics is discussed on a regular basis.

scheduling clerk. This person is responsible for scheduling the candidate's appointments and engagements. This person is responsible for handling any conflicting appointments and engagements. This person is also responsible for follow-ups and communicating to persons sponsoring events to which the candidate has been invited.

treasurer. This person is responsible for keeping an accurate record of donations and expenditures of the campaign.

voting district. The geographic area composed of the communities that a candidate is seeking to represent.

whisper campaign. A subtle, unspoken campaign based on negative innuendos. This type of campaign is used to create a negative image of a candidate.

Appendix F

Items to be a part of candidate's news kit

1. A statement of why candidate is seeking the particular office (one page)
2. A photo of candidate
3. A biography of candidate (one page)
4. Campaign platform, the candidate's statement of position on issues of the campaign (one page)
5. Copy of campaign brochure
6. Contact information for the candidate

Part II

Thoughts of an Elected Official

Appendix G

Glossary

body politics. A governmental body composed of elected official(s).

ghost write. A phrase used to refer to a writing that bears the authorship of one who is not the true author.

lobbyist. A person employed to advocate for a cause.

pet project. A favorite plan of an elected official used as a means to funnel money to a community.

redistribute wealth. A phrase used in reference to creating opportunities for acquiring wealth by those who do not normally have a reasonable chance to acquire wealth.

single issue. A term used in reference to an elected official having one cause that he seeks to use to govern.

www.ingramcontent.com/pod-product-compliance
Lightning Source LLC
Chambersburg PA
CBHW020538290526
45786CB00002B/933